This book belongs to :

Name: _______________

Family name: _______________

Age: _______________

A a is for Animals

A A a a a a

B b
is for
Bat

C C
is for
Cow

Dd

is for
Dolphin

E e *is for* **Egg**

Ff

is for
Fish

Gg
is for
Goat

H h *is for* Horse

Ii is for Ice cream

Jj is for
Jaguar

Kk
is for
Kangaroo

Ll

is for
Llama

Mm is for Mouse

N n *is for* Nest

N N n n n

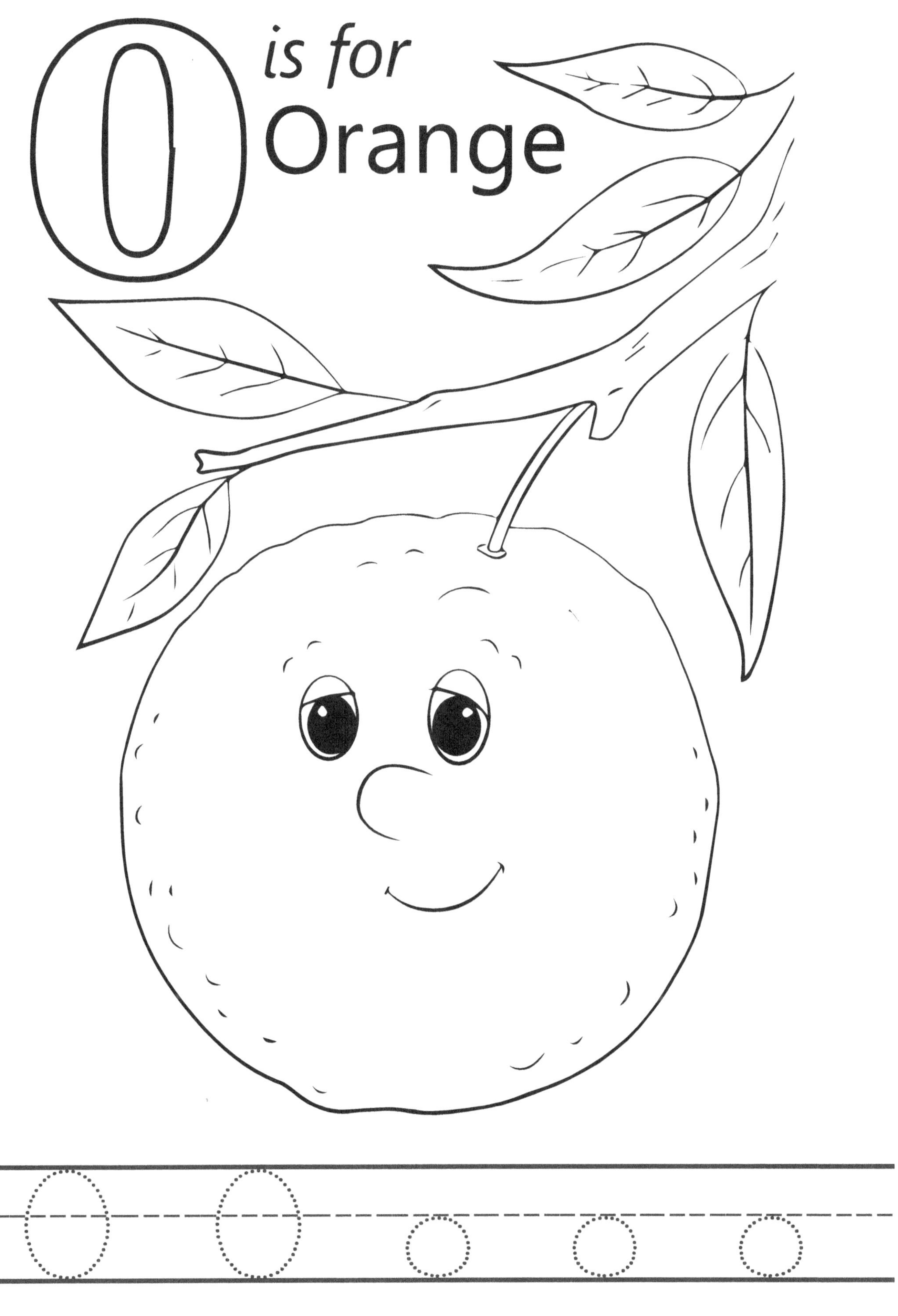

O
is for
Orange

P p
is for
Parrot

Qq is for Quail

R r

is for
Rabbit

S
is for
Spider

Tt

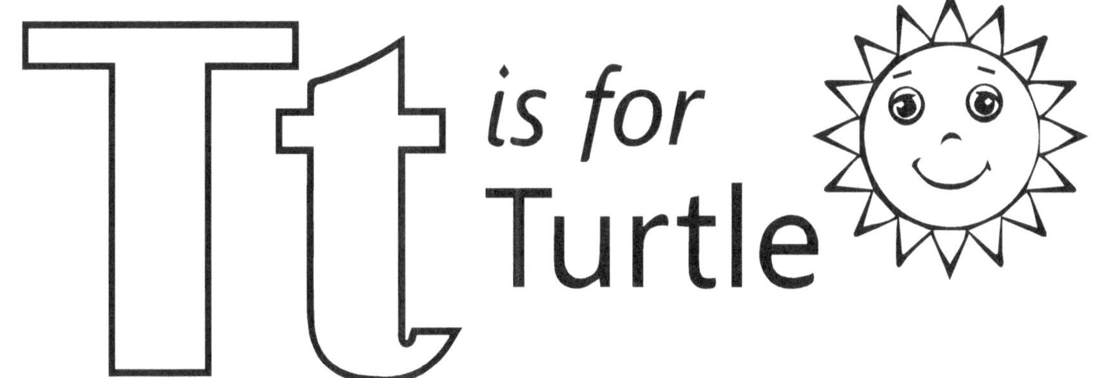

U u *is for*
Unicorn

V is for Vase

W
is for
Worm

X **is for**
Xylophone

Yy
is for Yak

Z